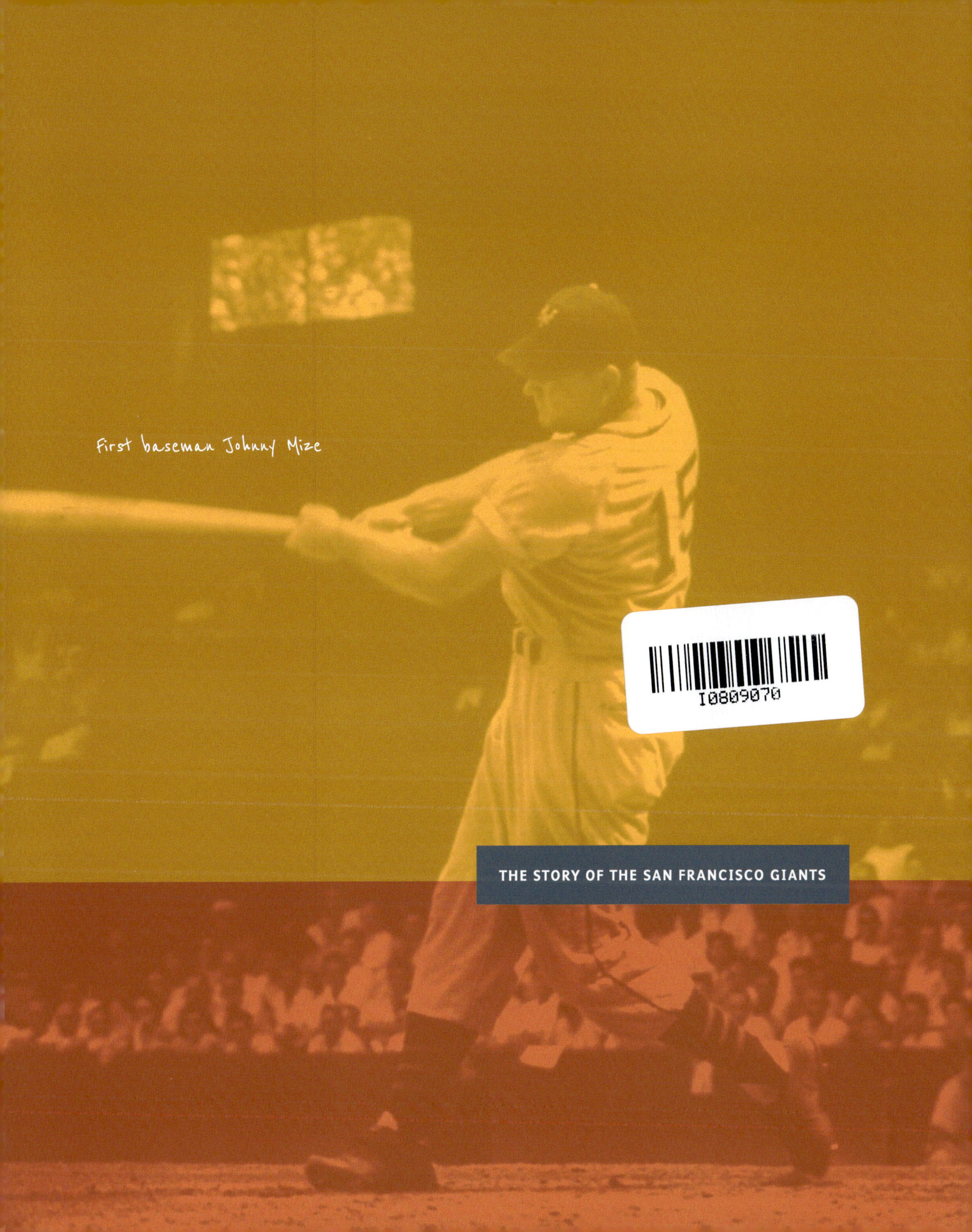

First baseman Johnny Mize

Pitcher Logan Webb

THE STORY OF THE

SAN FRANCISCO GIANTS

JIM WHITING

CREATIVE SPORTS

Catcher Buster Posey

CREATIVE EDUCATION / CREATIVE PAPERBACKS

Published by Creative Education and Creative Paperbacks
P.O. Box 227, Mankato, Minnesota 56002
Creative Education and Creative Paperbacks are imprints of
The Creative Company
www.thecreativecompany.us

Book Design by Wyeth Morgan
Art direction Blue Design (www.bluedes.com)

Images by Alamy Stock Photo/Albert Pena, 3; Associated Press/Anonymous, 11, Nick Wass, cover; Getty Images/B Bennett, 9, Bettmann, 10, 15, David Durochik/Diamond Images, 31, Dennis Desprois, 18, Diamond Images, 16, Don Smith, 6 (bottom, left), Focus On Sport, 7 (top, right), 19, Jane Tyska/MediaNews Group/East Bay Times, 2, JEFF HAYNES, 7 (bottom, right), Jed Jacobsohn, 22–23, 26–27, Keith Gillett/Icon Sportswire, 7 (bottom, left), Mark Rucker/Transcendental Graphics, 6 (top, left), 12, Mitchell Layton, 25, MONICA DAVEY, 6 (top, right), Nick Cammett/Diamond Images, 30, Ron Vesely, cover, 4–5, 32, Thearon W. Henderson, 29, Tomsic/WireImage, 20, W. Eugene Smith/Time Life Pictures, 1; Public Domain/7 (top, left); Wikimedia Commons/Goodwin & Company, 6 (bottom, right)

Library of Congress Cataloging-in-Publication Data
Names: Whiting, Jim, 1943- author
Title: The story of the San Francisco Giants / by Jim Whiting.
Description: Mankato, Minnesota : Creative Education and Creative Paperbacks, [2026] | Series: Creative sports. Major League baseball | Includes index. | Audience: Ages 8-12 | Audience: Grades 4-6 | Summary: "Discover the San Francisco Giants' thrilling journey from iconic moments like the "Shot Heard 'Round the World" to modern triumphs, featuring legendary players, and the Major League Baseball team's World Series victories. Written for middle-grade readers. Includes table of contents, sidebars, and index"– Provided by publisher.
Identifiers: LCCN 2025013124 (print) | LCCN 2025013125 (ebook) | ISBN 9798895811078 library binding | ISBN 9798896800606 paperback | ISBN 9798895812334 ebook
Subjects: LCSH: San Francisco Giants (Baseball team)–History–Juvenile literature.
Classification: LCC GV875.S34 W55 2026 (print) | LCC GV875.S34 (ebook) | DDC 796.357/640979461–dc23/eng/20250518
LC record available at https://lccn.loc.gov/2025013124
LC ebook record available at https://lccn.loc.gov/2025013125

Printed in the United States

First baseman Will Clark

GIANTS
Copyright 1888 by
GOODWIN & Co,
N.Y.

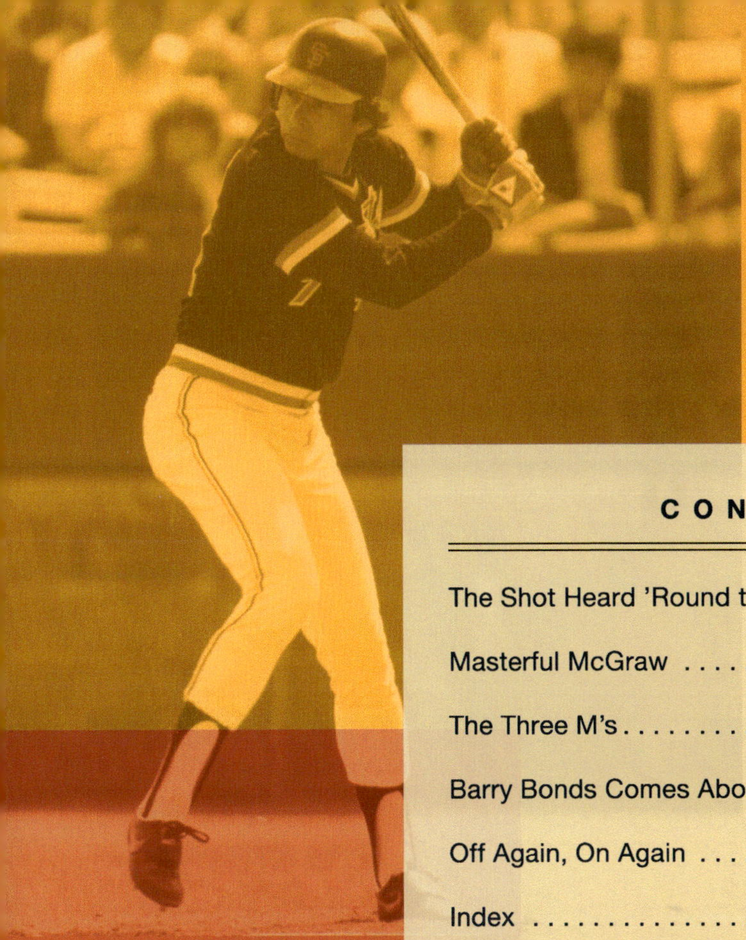

CONTENTS

EXTRA INNINGS

THE SHOT HEARD 'ROUND THE WORLD

On August 11, 1951, the New York Giants of Major League Baseball (MLB) lost their fourth game in a row. It dropped their season record to 59 wins, 51 losses. On the same day, the record of the Brooklyn Dodgers stood at 70–36. That gave the Dodgers a 13-game lead over the Giants in the National League (NL) pennant race. But the Giants weren't toast. They launched a 16-game winning streak that cut the margin to six games. They ended the season with a seven-game winning streak to finish with a 96–58 mark. During that time they went 37–7, an unbelievable 82 percent winning percentage. At the same time, Brooklyn went just 26–22 to finish with an identical 96–58 record.

That tie created a three-game playoff to determine which team would face the New York Yankees in the World Series. Giants third baseman Bobby Thomson smacked a two-run home run in the fourth inning of the first game. Left fielder Monte Irvin tacked on a solo shot in the eighth as New York won, 3–1. The Dodgers crushed the Giants 10–0 in Game 2. So whoever won Game 3 would win the pennant.

BALLS OUTS TEAM INNING TEAM INNING
BKLYN 1 0 0 0 0 0 0 3 0
N.Y. 0 0 0 0 0 0 1 0
UMPIRES PLATE 6
315 FT.

EXTRA INNINGS

BOBBY THOMSON
THIRD BASE, OUTFIELD
GIANTS SEASONS: 1946–53, 1957
HEIGHT: 6-FOOT-2
WEIGHT: 180 POUNDS
KEY STATS: .277 BATTING AVERAGE, 189 HOME RUNS, 704 RBIS, 3X ALL-STAR

THE STATEN ISLAND SCOT

Bobby Thomson was born in Scotland and moved with his family to the New York borough of Staten Island when he was three. He signed a contract with the Giants for $100 in 1942 when he graduated from high school. He played briefly in the low minor leagues, then served in the Army Air Corps for several years. Thomson joined the Giants at the end of the 1946 season. He had a solid career in New York, with six seasons of at least 20 home runs and 3 All-Star selections. But he will always be remembered for his renowned 1951 home run. "It was the best thing that ever happened to me," he said years later. "It may have been the best thing that ever happened to anybody."

The Giants win the pennant!

Brooklyn led 4–1 going into the bottom of the ninth. Giants shortstop Alvin Dark led off with a single. Right fielder Don Mueller also singled. Irvin popped out. First baseman Whitey Lockman doubled to left-center field. Dark easily scored. Mueller slid into third base. Thomson stepped up to the plate to face Brooklyn pitcher Ralph Branca. "If you ever hit one [a home run], hit it now," Giants manager Leo Durocher told him. Thomson had hit a career-high 31 long balls during the regular season.

"[Branca] threw the first pitch right down the middle, and I took it," Thomson said. "The guys told me later, when I took that first pitch right down the middle, they literally wanted to kill me!" It was a good pitch to hit.

"Then Ralph tried to waste the second pitch, to set me up, you know, for a breaking ball on the third pitch," Thomson continued. "But I was quick with my hands. I had been hitting quite well, and I got around on it."

The ball flew deep into left field. It dropped into the stands for a three-run home run. The Giants won, 5–4! Thomson danced around the bases as Giants sportscaster Russ Hodges screamed into his microphone, "The Giants win the pennant! ... I don't believe it! I do not believe it!"

Thomson's blast is one of the most famous home runs in MLB history. *The Sporting News* ranked it number one on its 1999 list of Greatest Baseball Moments. It acquired its enduring nickname of "the shot heard 'round the world." That is an echo of the phrase used to describe the start of the American Revolutionary War on April 19, 1775.

MASTERFUL MCGRAW

The Giants were established in 1883. At first, they were called the Gothams, which is a nickname for New York City. Early in the 1885 season, a newspaper game report referred to the team as "Giants." The new name quickly caught on.

The Giants won the NL pennant in 1888 and 1889. During the 1890s, pitcher Amos Rusie won 20 or more games in eight different seasons. But the team dropped in the league standings. Feisty infielder John McGraw joined the team during the 1902 season as player/manager. His gruff manner earned him the nickname "Little Napoleon." Like the notorious French emperor, he had great ambition and self-confidence. "The main idea is to win," he said. "I think we can win it if my brain holds out."

McGraw pushed the Giants to a 106–47 record in 1904. It remained the franchise record for wins for more than a century. Pitcher Joe McGinnity won 35 games. Crafty Christy Mathewson added 33. The team captured the NL pennant. But the Giants refused to play the American League (AL) champion Boston Americans in the World Series, which had begun the previous year.

Infielder John McGraw

Both McGraw and owner John T. Brush considered the league inferior. The NL dated back to 1876. The AL was in just its fourth major-league season.

The Giants relented the next season. They faced the AL's Philadelphia Athletics in the World Series. Mathewson threw three complete-game shutouts. New York won the championship, four games to one. "Mathewson was the greatest pitcher who ever lived," said Athletics manager Connie Mack. "It was wonderful to watch him pitch—when he wasn't pitching against you."

The team captured pennants in 1911, 1912, and 1913. Yet the Giants came up short in the World Series each time. In 1916, they won a major-league record 26 games in a row. But they finished fourth. Mathewson left the team. He had an NL-record 373 wins. All but one were with the Giants. New York returned to the top of the league in 1917. Again, they lost the World Series.

Clutch-hitting outfielder Irish Meusel and speedy infielder Frankie Frisch sparked the team in the early 1920s. The Giants won the NL pennant from 1921 to 1924. They topped the New York Yankees in the 1921 and 1922 World Series. But the Yankees beat them in the next "Fall Classic." In the 1924 World Series, the Giants fell to the Washington Senators.

New York continued to post winning records. But it fell short of the pennant. The Giants dropped to sixth place in 1932. McGraw retired in midseason. His win total of 2,763 games remains second only to Connie Mack's 3,731.

First baseman Bill Terry replaced McGraw as player/manager. Several star players joined the team in the late 1920s and early '30s. One was right fielder Mel Ott. He hit 511 home runs in 22 years with the Giants. "King Carl" Hubbell and "Prince Hal" Schumacher led the pitching staff for more than a decade. The Giants captured the pennant again in 1933. They defeated the Senators

EXTRA INNINGS

BIRTH OF A RIVALRY

The New York Giants won the NL pennant in 1889. Then they faced the American Association-winning Brooklyn Bridegrooms. The matchup was a 19th-century version of the World Series. The Giants won. It marked the beginning of one of the greatest rivalries in professional sports. The Bridegrooms joined the NL in 1890 and later changed their name to Dodgers. The two teams have engaged in many exciting pennant races since then. In 1925, Brooklyn's team president Charles Ebbets died the morning a Giants-Dodgers series was scheduled to begin. The games went on. Brooklyn manager Wilbert Robinson said, "Charlie wouldn't want anybody to miss a Giants-Brooklyn series just because he died." In 1956, the unthinkable happened. The Dodgers traded Jackie Robinson—who had broken the color barrier in baseball in 1947 and became a star for nearly a decade—to the Giants. Robinson retired rather than suiting up for the hated Giants.

EXTRA INNINGS

WILLIE MAYS
CENTER FIELDER
GIANTS SEASONS:
1951–52, 1954–72
HEIGHT: 5-FOOT-10
WEIGHT: 170 POUNDS
KEY STATS: .304 BATTING AVERAGE, 646 HOME RUNS, 1,859 RBIS, 336 STOLEN BASES

THE GREATEST EVER?

Willie Mays was the original five-tool player. He fielded brilliantly. He made laser throws. He stole bases, hit for high averages, and had power. At age 20, he hit .274 with 20 home runs and 68 runs batted in (RBIs). He was named Rookie of the Year. Three years later, he earned his first of two Most Valuable Player (MVP) awards. He also made the first of 19 consecutive All-Star appearances. The 12-time Gold Glove winner ended his career as the first player with 600 homers, 300 stolen bases, and 3,000 hits. "He had that other ingredient that turns a superstar into a super superstar. He lit up the room when he came in. He was a joy to be around," said manager Leo Durocher.

in the World Series. They won the pennant again in 1936 and 1937. Both times, they fell to the Yankees in the World Series.

THE THREE M'S

From 1938 to 1950, New York never finished above third. The 1951 season seemed like yet another disappointing finish before Thomson's dramatic home run. But the Giants lost to the Yankees in six games in the World Series.

Young superstar center fielder Willie Mays led New York to another pennant in 1954. The team swept the Cleveland Indians in the World Series. New York fans got to watch Mays for only a few more years. Owner Horace Stoneham moved the team to San Francisco before the 1958 season. Stoneham hoped to build a larger fan base there.

The Giants welcomed several new players to their West Coast home. One was Rookie of the Year first baseman Orlando Cepeda. Later, Cepeda shifted to the outfield. That made room for Willie McCovey at first base. He was named Rookie of the Year in 1959. McCovey displayed fearsome hitting and graceful fielding.

In 1960, the Giants moved into Candlestick Park. The stadium was located on the western shore of San Francisco Bay. Fly balls were often swept up in the swirling winds. That made it difficult for outfielders to catch them. A new pitching star emerged midway through the season. Rookie Juan Marichal kicked his leg high in the air when he pitched.

The three M's—Mays, McCovey, and Marichal—formed the core of an NL powerhouse. The Giants surged to 103 wins in 1962. They won the pennant by

First baseman Willie McCovey

one game. San Francisco battled through seven games in the World Series. The trophy went to its old rival, the Yankees.

San Francisco spent the rest of the 1960s near the top of the NL. Mays continued to thrill fans with his booming bat and slick fielding. McCovey ranked among the league's home run leaders. Marichal continued his dominance of opposing batters. But the team always fell short of the pennant. In 1969, the NL split into two divisions. The Giants joined the West Division. They edged out the Dodgers for the division crown in 1971. In the postseason, the Giants quickly fell to the Pittsburgh Pirates.

During the next 15 years, the Giants enjoyed numerous high points. But they failed to reach the playoffs. The team hit rock bottom in 1985, losing 100 games. Former Giants pitcher Roger Craig took over as manager. "We're going to get back to the basics," Craig announced. "If we can discipline ourselves to do the little things right, the big things will take care of themselves."

Craig blended youngsters and veterans. His methods brought success in 1987. The team won its first division title since 1971. It took the lead in the National League Championship Series (NLCS) against the St. Louis Cardinals.

Center fielder Willie Mays

EXTRA INNINGS

JUAN MARICHAL
PITCHER
GIANTS SEASONS: 1960–73
HEIGHT: 6-FOOT-0
WEIGHT: 185 POUNDS
KEY STATS: 238–140 WIN-LOSS RECORD, 2.84 EARNED RUN AVERAGE, 2281 STRIKEOUTS, 9X ALL-STAR

THE DOMINICAN DANDY

Juan Marichal gave an indication of what was to come in his first start with the Giants. He pitched a one-hit shutout. During the next 12 seasons, he won at least 20 games six times. His 238 wins are the third-most in Giants history. The most notable win came in 1963. Marichal and Warren Spahn of the Milwaukee Braves each threw 15 innings of shutout ball. Marichal kept the string going in the top of the 16th before Mays cracked a walk-off home run in the bottom half of the inning. David Adler of mlb.com called it "the greatest game ever pitched." Marichal also notched the first Giants no-hitter since 1929 that season. In 1983, he became the first player from the Dominican Republic elected to the Baseball Hall of Fame.

But St. Louis threw two shutouts to win the series. Two years later, San Francisco topped the NL West again. It defeated the Chicago Cubs in the NLCS. The Giants faced the Oakland Athletics in the "Bay Bridge World Series." The Giants lost the first two games. Minutes before Game 3, a major earthquake rocked the area. The Series was postponed for 10 days. The Giants never recovered. They lost the Series in four games.

BARRY BONDS COMES ABOARD

San Francisco began a downward spiral in the 1990s. Then Pittsburgh Pirates left fielder Barry Bonds signed a free-agent contract before the 1993 season. Bonds had deep ties to the Giants. His father Bobby had been a two-time All-Star with the Giants in the late '60s and early '70s. Mays was his godfather. Bonds showcased his awesome skills with 46 homers and 123 runs batted in (RBIs). He also stole 29 bases. The Giants won 103 games. They missed the NL West title by a single game.

The team remained near the top of the standings for much of the 1990s. Second baseman Jeff Kent and first baseman J. T. Snow arrived in 1997. The Giants won the division title that season and again three years later. They failed to reach the World Series each time.

Bonds ushered in the new millennium with unprecedented power. In 2001, he slammed an MLB-record 73 homers. He drove in 137 runs. His batting average was .328. "This was one of the greatest years—no, it was the greatest year—I have seen from a single person," said manager Dusty Baker. The next year, Bonds led the league with a .370 batting average. He helped

GIANTS
neweraca
neweraca
Bank of Americ
47

Outfielder Barry Bonds

propel the Giants to a Wild Card berth. The team advanced to the World Series. It lost a seven-game battle to the Anaheim Angels.

Bonds helped the Giants to another NL West title in 2003. He earned his fourth straight MVP award the following year. He retired in 2007 as baseball's all-time home run king with a total of 762 with the Pirates and Giants. Bonds also established a record for walks with 2,558. Nearly 700 were intentional. Rather than face his powerful bat, opposing teams often opted to give him free passes.

The Giants posted losing records from 2006 to 2008. But help was on the way from young pitchers Matt Cain and Tim Lincecum, veteran center fielder Aaron Rowand, and rookie third baseman Pablo Sandoval.

The newcomers helped the Giants improve to 88–74 in 2009. In 2010, the team won a tight battle for the NL West. Catcher Buster Posey was Rookie of the Year. San Francisco flattened the Atlanta Braves and Philadelphia Phillies in the playoffs. It faced the Texas Rangers in the World Series. The Giants won in five games. It was their first world championship since 1954.

OFF AGAIN, ON AGAIN

The Giants missed the playoffs in 2011. They won the pennant the following season. Posey hit .336 for the NL batting title. He was named the league's MVP. San Francisco faced the Detroit Tigers in the World Series. Sandoval smashed three dingers in Game 1. San Francisco cruised to an 8–3 win. Its pitching staff recorded shutouts in the next two games. The Giants swept the series with a 4–3 Game 4 victory.

Third baseman Pablo Sandoval

SAN FRANCISCO

EXTRA INNINGS

TIM LINCECUM
PITCHER
GIANTS SEASONS: 2007–15
HEIGHT: 5-FOOT-11
WEIGHT: 170 POUNDS
KEY STATS: 198–83 WINS-LOSSES, 3.61 EARNED RUN AVERAGE, 1,704 STRIKEOUTS, 4X ALL-STAR

FREAK SHOW

After his senior year in high school, Tim Lincecum was chosen in the 48th round of the 2003 MLB Draft. He chose to play for the University of Washington instead. It was a good decision. In 2006 he won the Golden Spikes Award as the best amateur player in the United States. The Giants took him 10th overall in the MLB draft. He was nicknamed "The Freak" because of his unusual pitching motion. "It looks like his head is going to snap off and his arm is going to fly off," said Cleveland general manager Mark Shapiro. Lincecum became a power pitcher and won the Cy Young Award in 2008 and 2009. He is the first pitcher to win the award in his first two full MLB seasons. He led the league in strikeouts in 2008, 2009, and 2010. He pitched no-hitters in 2013 and 2014. "For an all-too-brief time, the pitcher who didn't look or throw like anybody else could pitch better than everybody else," said Nick Selbe of *Sports Illustrated*.

San Francisco was back in the playoffs in 2014 after finishing 88–74. It easily defeated the Pirates in the Wild Card game. Then it romped through the next two rounds of playoffs. The Giants faced the Kansas City Royals in the World Series. The Giants won the championship in a tense Game 7. It was their third Series win in five years.

San Francisco missed the playoffs in 2015. The team's year-on, year-off pattern continued in 2016. The Giants were second in the NL West. The Wild Card game against the New York Mets was scoreless through eight innings. In the top of the ninth, little-used infielder Conor Gillaspie smacked a three-run homer. Pitching ace Madison Bumgarner completed the shutout. But they lost to the Cubs in the National League Division Series (NLDS), three games to one.

The team got off to a slow start in 2017. Then Bumgarner was injured. The Giants finished at 64–98. It was their worst record in terms of win-loss percentage since 1985. The following season was similar. Bumgarner was hurt again. So were several other players. The Giants improved slightly to 73–89. Their 77–85 finish in 2019 was the third straight year under .500. Jeff Samardzija was the only pitcher to win more than nine games.

In 2020, the Giants went 29–31 in a shortened season due to the COVID-19 pandemic. That record tied them with the Milwaukee Brewers for the eighth and final playoff spot. The Brewers advanced because they had a better record within their division.

The Giants broke out of the slump in a big way in 2021. They went 107–55. It was the best record in MLB that season. It was also the team's best-ever record, breaking the old mark of 106 wins that dated back to 1904. One of the main reasons for the comeback was Posey's return after sitting out the

EXTRA INNINGS

MADISON BUMGARNER
PITCHER
GIANTS SEASONS: 2009–19
HEIGHT: 6-FOOT-4
WEIGHT: 240 POUNDS
KEY STATS: 119–92 WIN-LOSS RECORD, 3.47 EARNED RUN AVERAGE, 1,794 STRIKEOUTS, 4X ALL-STAR

MADISON THE MAGNIFICENT

Madison Bumgarner dominated Game 1 of the 2014 World Series against the Kansas City Royals. He allowed only one run in seven innings. He threw a complete-game shutout in Game 5. In Game 7, the Giants held a 3–2 lead after four innings. They called on Bumgarner even though he had just two days of rest rather than the usual four or five for starting pitchers. He carried that narrow lead into the bottom of the ninth. Bumgarner retired the first two hitters. The third Kansas City batter drove the ball into left-center field. Outfielder Gregor Blanco misplayed the ball and it rolled to the fence. The batter wound up on third base. With the tying run just 90 feet away, Bumgarner induced the next Royals batter to pop up for the final out. He became the first pitcher since 1909 to start two World Series games and make a relief appearance of more than three innings in a third game. He was named World Series MVP.

Rawlings

Shortstop Willy Adames

previous season. He provided veteran leadership and batted .304, nearly 50 points higher than in 2019. Gabe Kapler was named Manager of the Year. The Giants faced the Dodgers in the NLDS. They took two of the first three games. But they managed just three runs in the next two games as the Dodgers took the series, three games to two.

The Giants couldn't maintain that momentum. The next three seasons were virtually identical. They won 81 games in 2022, 79 the following season, and 80 in 2024.

For more than 135 years, the Giants have thrilled fans. Their history includes dozens of Baseball Hall of Fame inductees and eight world championships. Those figures are sure to rise in years to come. Giants fans look forward to more World Series crowns in the future.

Outfielder Heliot Ramos

INDEX